For my daughter, ~~Azalea~~ Annika, as she starts the next chapter in her life.

Embrace The Suck

verb, military slang

To conciously accept or appreciate something that is extremely unpleasant but unavoidable for forward progression. DKI

love you Shate I'm So Proud of you! Love Papa

UNDERSTAND LIFE ISN'T FAIR

I am going to start out with this one because it is a simple truth a lot of adults fail to accept.

Imagine playing a board game that gives every participant a different set of rules. Some start with more money. Others start further up the board or get additional turns. And, as much as it pains me to say it, some players will receive penalties simply because of the color of their skin and/or gender. That is how life works.

The best advice I can give regarding this is to do the best you can with the set of rules you were handed. Try to re-write some of them if you have the opportunity but, instead of focusing on winning, just try to have as much fun as you can.

KNOW YOUR CORE VALUES

Adulthood is full of compromises. Knowing which things you value most will make it easier for you to know when to draw the line on those compromises. It is also important to remember core values do sometimes change. Take the time to reevaluate your priorities and beliefs on a regular basis.

Stand tall & proud, the
Blood of Vikings Runs
in your veins
Great Great Grandma
Daniels

LIFE DOESN'T STOP JUST BECAUSE YOU DO

One other harsh reality about life is it has a time limit but you aren't allowed to see the clock. While it is OK to take a break whenever you feel overwhelmed, it is also important to remember that the clock will continue to run.

Don't assume there will be a tomorrow and don't put off the important things for longer than necessary. Again, it's fine to take a break if you need one. Just remember, even though you are calling "time out," nobody is stopping that game clock.

FIND SOMETHING THAT GIVES YOU A SENSE OF PURPOSE

This doesn't need to be your career. It can be volunteer time at a favorite non-profit, being active in your church, time spent with a favorite hobby or even something as simple as raising a family. Whatever you choose, make sure it is something that makes you excited to get out of bed each morning.

MAKE AN EFFORT TO BE A KIND PERSON

Compliments and words of encouragement cost you nothing, so be generous with them. You never know when a simple kind word will turn someone's day around.

Don't take pleasure in someone else's misfortune, even if that person might be the kind of person who deserves it. Instead, treat them the way you would want to be treated if you found yourself in a similar situation because, some day, you might.

The world can be a cruel place. If people can remember you as being one of the few exceptions, that's not such a bad thing.

LACK OF SUCCESS ISN'T THE SAME AS FAILING

You won't succeed at everything you set out to do. In fact, odds are you will not succeed at most things you try, at least not at first.

Embrace these moments as a learning experience and, while you analyze what went wrong, also make sure to give yourself credit for the things that went right and build on that.

More importantly, take the time to remember that everyone falls flat on their face at some point in their life. Falling doesn't make you a failure.

Choosing not to get back up after the fall does.

DON'T RELY ON OTHER PEOPLE TO MAKE YOU HAPPY

The only person who can really make you happy is you. Your friends, family, romantic partners, etc., will amplify that happiness but you have to be the one who gets the ball rolling.

Start each morning by looking in the mirror and finding something you like about yourself, whether it is a physical trait or something else. Build on that each day and you'll find you have a lot of things in your life to be happy for, even without outside help. In contrast to that, miserable people will always be miserable, regardless of how many good and caring people they have in their life.

BEING ANGRY ABOUT THE RAIN DOESN'T MAKE IT GO AWAY

There will be things that happen in your life that you don't like but also will not be able to change. It's natural to want to feel angry about those things but don't let that anger turn into a waste of time and effort.

Instead, be quick to accept what you cannot change so you can focus on working around the problem. Turn your angry energy into productive energy.

DON'T LET ROUGH PATCHES DEFEAT YOU BUT DO LET THEM HUMBLE YOU

There have been times when I've had to scrape up every penny just to buy a meal and those times made me appreciate the times when I had enough money to buy a little extra. It also made it easier to feel empathy for others who may be going through similar circumstances. You may or may not go through similar circumstances but, if you do, make sure it makes a positive impression on you.

NEGATIVE THINKING USUALLY LEADS TO NEGATIVE RESULTS

One "trick" people like to use to avoid disappointment is to assume the worst will happen. That way, when they don't succeed, it was expected.

While it seems like a sound strategy on paper, negative thinking also has the potential to cause us to subconsciously sabotage ourselves, creating a never-ending loop of disappointment.

Instead of focusing on the worst that could happen, focus, instead, on the positive things you know are true - "I am faster today than the last time I ran this race," "I am better prepared for this test than the last test," "I like this restaurant so, even if the date doesn't go well, I'll have a good meal."

Positive thinking doesn't guarantee positive results but will give you a better chance at succeeding. Disappointment hurts whether you expected it or not so why not put yourself in the best position to avoid it?

SOME PEOPLE JUST DON'T WANT TO BE SAVED

Imagine you are on a sinking ship. If you have an opportunity to escort others to the lifeboats, you should. However, if one of those people refuses to leave, the decision to help becomes a lot more complicated.

That's the way life is as well. You should want to help but should be careful not to spend a lot of time trying to rescue someone who doesn't want to be saved. Otherwise, you might wind up drowning with them.

PROCRASTINATION CAN BE
HABIT-FORMING

Once you come up with a reason to delay doing
something, it becomes surprisingly easy to come up
with other reasons to avoid doing it even longer.
That doesn't even include the number of things
outside your control that might pop up.
Don't fall into this trap. Just like any other
addiction,it will eventually come back to hurt you.

NOT GETTING YOUR WAY DOESN'T MEAN YOU ARE A VICTIM

A lot of adults struggle with this concept.
Sometimes, no matter how hard you try, you don't win. There's nothing wrong with that, it's just part of life.
Don't walk around acting like you are a victim as a result of this. There are plenty of people in the world who really are victims and you would just be insulting them.

A BROWN NOSER'S VIEW NEVER CHANGES

The problem with achieving success by mastering the art of flattery is, ultimately, you are always going to need to rely on another person to help you move up the ladder. Plus, it's very hard to get the respect from your peers if you are perceived as someone who didn't advance because of your own merits. Put in the hard work and make yourself irreplaceable. It's a strategy that might take you a bit longer but also creates unlimited potential for you. Not to mention you'll have a lot more respect for yourself and from others.

NOT EVERYONE WHO IS NICE TO YOU IS YOUR FRIEND

Human beings crave companionship, even those of us who are introverts. Unfortunately, because of that, it is sometimes easy to be blinded to someone's real nature and think they are a friend when they aren't.

Over time, it becomes a bit easier to recognize the people who are really your friends and those who are only using you for their own personal gain. In the meantime, try to be selective about who you share your innermost secrets with.

An easy shortcut - tell your "friend" something they don't want to hear. More often than not, they'll reveal their true self to you as a result.

IT'S EASY TO SECOND-GUESS DECISIONS WHEN YOU'RE NOT THE ONE IN THE DRIVER'S SEAT

People like to question someone else's decisions when they don't have or understand all the facts leading to that decision. Be aware of this and don't let their criticism of your decisions influence you because, whether you were right or wrong, they weren't the ones who were forced to make a difficult choice at that time.

Also keep this in mind when evaluating the decisions of others. Even if they made the wrong choice, assume they made it based on the information they had at the time and treat them with the respect they deserve.

PEER PRESSURE STILL EXISTS WHEN YOU'RE AN ADULT

It'll be about different things, like getting married, having kids, buying a house or getting a better job, but the concept is basically the same as when you were in middle school and high school.
The advice for this is the same - make your decisions based on what you want and not what your friends want and don't do anything that makes you uncomfortable. In other words, be your own person regardless of what everyone else wants you to do.

OFFICE SUPPLIES ALWAYS MAKE A GREAT GIFT

One thing that surprised me about being an adult was just how many gifts I get stuck buying each year. It might be something for a distant cousin's graduation or a co-worker's birthday and, if you end up in a serious relationship, the number doubles. Everyone needs pens, stationary, and various other objects that can be found at your local office supply store. It's an easy gift in a pinch that requires very little personalization.

Along those lines, first aid kids and fire extinguishers are great gifts for people with kids. I have yet to meet a single parent who didn't think they wouldn't use them.

IT IS OK TO ORDER THE SAME THING OFF THE MENU EVERY TIME

Should you be willing to try new things? Of course. However, regardless of what people might try to tell you, there is also nothing wrong with knowing what you like and choosing something you are familiar with. This is especially true if you are the one paying for it.

JUST BECAUSE YOU HAVE THE SAME GOAL AS SOMEONE ELSE DOESN'T MEAN YOU'RE ALLIES

This is a lesson I've learned after sitting on many committees. Sometimes, you can be in 100 percent agreement with a person (or group of people) about what you want to accomplish but disagree on every single other thing.

This scenario is surprisingly common and rarely productive. If you really want to accomplish your goal, you are better off walking away and starting over, assuming you are able to.

THE BEST PRICE ISN'T ALWAYS THE BEST VALUE

This is another one of those concepts people sometimes struggle with. Being the least expensive doesn't guarantee a subpar product but, more often than not, a significant price difference could be the result of you giving something up in return.

This could be a lot of things - already assembled versus assembly required, warranty versus no warranty, good customer service versus no customer service, 2-day shipping versus "you'll get it eventually."

Know what is important to you and always read the fine print before making a purchase based on the price tag.

MORE EXPENSIVE DOESN'T ALWAYS MEAN BETTER QUALITY

On the flip side of what I just said, if something is more expensive, don't assume the higher price means it is the better product.
Sure, sometimes it might be. Other times, it might just be because you're paying for the more expensive packaging. Once again, do your research and make an informed decision.

ALWAYS LISTEN TO EXPERT ADVICE WITH A HINT OF SKEPTICISM

I'm not saying the experts are always wrong or that they would intentionally try to mislead you. I am just saying having the title of "expert" doesn't necessarily make you right 100 percent of the time. Doctors used to promote the health benefits of cigarettes and, not that long ago, experts were telling us plastic shopping bags would save the environment.

They are considered "experts" for a reason and give them respect for that. Just don't take everything they tell you as gospel.

PRACTICE MARKETING YOURSELF

It doesn't need to be a daily thing, but make sure to take time in front of the mirror and review your strengths and various attributes. There will be plenty of times in your life when you will need to be able to do this, whether it is a job interview or first date. It is also a great way to feel better about yourself if you are ever feeling a bit down.

BEING FIRST ISN'T ALWAYS A GOOD THING

There are certain situations when it is sometimes best to let people go ahead of you. This includes, but is not limited to, buying new technology, trying the latest "miracle" drug, and even paying to see the newest blockbuster film.

As you get older, use your experiences to figure out when you should push your way to the front and when you should just hang back and let others cut in line.

WRITE THINGS DOWN

We all like to think we can remember something as simple as a 3-item shopping list or the title of a book we want to check out at the library. Unfortunately, that's just not the case, especially as you get older and have a lot more things you need to remember too.

Take a few seconds to write it on a slip of paper or as a memo in your phone. You may be right and you may not actually need the reminder but it's still better than needing to make a second trip.

LEARN TO SEPARATE FACT FROM OPINION

This might sound easy but the world has gotten very good at making these two things difficult to distinguish. More than ever, it is important to take the time to get to know more about your source so you can recognize bias and be able to determine how much of their "fact" is actually factual.

SOMETIMES YOU NEED TO ADDRESS THE SYMPTOMS BEFORE ADDRESSING THE CAUSE

When firefighters arrive at a burning building, they may want to know what started the fire but will first make sure to extinguish the flames before they do any more damage. A lot of things in life are going to be like that as well. You may want to address the root of a specific problem but also shouldn't ignore the immediate and damaging issues that stem from that underlying problem.

IF IT REQUIRES A TIME COMMITMENT, THEN IT ISN'T REALLY "FREE"

As you get older, you'll discover there are a lot of people who want to give you "free" meals, vacations, kitchenware, etc. in exchange for listening to a sales pitch or demonstration. However, if you are committing more than a few minutes of your time, then it isn't really free. That's not to say you shouldn't take advantage of some of those offers. You might get a good meal out of it or even a nice weekend getaway. Just make sure you are treating your time as an asset and the reward you are getting is worth the commitment you are making.

JUDGE "LOVE" BY ACTIONS NOT WORDS

Anyone can say three words. The people who really love you are the ones who back up those words with their actions.

Do they bring you soup when you're sick? Do they remember your birthday and important anniversaries? Do they do things they dislike because you enjoy them? Pay close attention to these things because, on occasion, you might discover someone who cares for you but is too afraid to express it in words.

It should also go without saying, if someone mistreats you, either physically or emotionally, they don't love you, no matter how many times they claim they do. Walk away from those relationships quickly and with your head held high.

UNHEALTHY HABITS ARE A BIT LIKE BUYING ON CREDIT

Your body may not have to pay for them now, while you're young but, much like interest on a credit card or loan, the damage from bad habits accrues and your body will eventually need to pay that bill.
It's OK to "splurge" a bit with some junk food and days when you just lie around doing nothing. Just make sure to balance that out with healthy meals and exercise to delay and reduce the inevitable balloon payment that will be waiting for you when you get older.

ONLY A FEW DAYS WILL RESULT SOME SORT OF ADVENTURE BUT THAT DOESN'T MEAN THE OTHERS CAN'T BE LIFE CHANGING

You may not realize it when it happens but even a "normal" day could have a major impact on the rest of your life, whether it is a chance meeting at the grocery store or a seemingly insignificant decision, like turning left instead of right. Remember to treat each day with the respect it deserves because you never know if it will be the day that alters your life forever.

DON'T LET UNFULFILLED DREAMS BLIND YOU TO THE GOOD THINGS IN YOUR LIFE

Sometimes we want something so bad, it makes anything less seem like a failure. Don't let that unfulfilled desire lessen the impact of what you have already done.

If you have good health, a roof over your head, food on the table, and people who love you, be both proud and grateful for that. There are a lot of people out there that would love to have what you already have.

In fact, you might even say your life is likely someone else's unfulfilled dream.

SOMETIMES ALL IT TAKES TO GET MOTIVATED IS GETTING DRESSED

Everyone has days when they don't want to get out of bed and do the things that are on their list. On these days, finding motivation will likely be much more difficult than others.

Obviously, staying in bed isn't always going to be an option, especially if you have bills to pay. My advice is to start small and force yourself to get dressed. Once you are up and moving, motivation to do other things often follows.

HAVING A CONTINGENCY PLAN DOESN'T MAKE YOU A PESSIMIST

There is nothing wrong with setting aside money for emergency use or figuring out a step-by-step game plan for a worst case scenario and keeping it in your back pocket.

Some people might consider you a pessimist but, if anything, having a sound emergency plan makes it much easier to take chances and try new things. It'll also make your life less stressful knowing you will be able to bounce back if you ever hit rock bottom.

IT'S OK TO CHANGE FOR A PERSON YOU CARE ABOUT AS LONG AS YOU AREN'T THE ONLY ONE

Actually, I don't like the word "change" in this context so I'll use the word "grow" instead. If you meet someone who makes you want to grow as an individual, including taking up new interests, that's not necessarily a bad thing.
Just make sure they are willing to grow too. Otherwise, you'll eventually outgrow the relationship.

A LOT OF TIMES YOUR TONE OF VOICE WILL HAVE MORE OF AN IMPACT THAN THE WORDS YOU ARE SAYING

This can hurt or help you depending on the situation and is something you should pay close attention to when having a conversation with someone else. It's also something that is worth taking the time to practice if you need to make a speech, have a job interview, or are expecting another situation where someone might misinterpret your message based on how they think you sound.

INSTEAD OF FOCUSING ON "WHAT MIGHT HAVE BEEN," FOCUS ON "WHAT CAN STILL HAPPEN"

A lot of people waste a very large chunk of their lives living in regret of decisions they made in their past. Don't be one of those people.
Instead, learn from your mistakes but leave the past where it belongs and focus on the future. There are a lot of good things that can still happen to you if you don't waste your time imagining an alternate timeline that didn't happen.

JUST BECAUSE A DOOR CLOSED DOESN'T MEAN IT IS LOCKED

And just because another door opened doesn't mean you can't try to reopen the closed door first. I'm not saying this will be the best choice in all situations but if that first door leads to something you really want out of life, it won't hurt to test the doorknob a couple times, just to make sure.

ASSIGNING BLAME IS ONE OF THE LEAST PRODUCTIVE THINGS YOU CAN DO IN A CRISIS

Granted, it is easier to figure out who to point fingers at. However, that also ultimately does very little to solve the problem.

Focus your time and energy on resolving the issue first. Then, if there's still time, you can figure out who was responsible for the problem to begin with or, better, you can let the history books determine who was at fault.

GLOBAL CHANGE STARTS AT THE COMMUNITY LEVEL

Changing the world starts with changing your own little piece of it first. If you really want to change the world for the better, start by finding ways to make your community better.

Volunteer at a homeless shelter, run a food drive for the needy, spend time each week picking up garbage off the ground, give blood on a regular basis, or become active in groups that are working to make lives better. Those things will have more of an impact than you may ever realize.

VOLUNTEERING CAN BECOME ADDICTIVE

Doing something good for your community can have a positive impact on your mental health, especially if you feel appreciated for your efforts. This, in turn, can make you want to volunteer more. However, as with all good things, make sure to know your limitations and find a healthy balance. If you spend all your time volunteering, you won't be able to live your life or pay your bills. There is nothing wrong with just making a monetary donation every once in a while.

TRY TO ALWAYS KEEP THINGS IN PERSPECTIVE

A 50-degree day might feel cold after a hot summer but will feel much warmer after a long winter. Life is a bit like that too.

A bad moment is just a single moment out of many and you shouldn't let it ruin an entire day. On the other end of the spectrum, an accomplishment shouldn't be a reason to stop trying to achieve more. Your worst day could always be worse and your best day could always be better.

THE LESSER OF TWO EVILS IS STILL EVIL

As adults, we are often asked to choose between the lesser of two evils. This is especially true during election time, when many will try to convince you there isn't another choice.

Before choosing, always take the time to verify there isn't a third option that doesn't fall into the "evil" category. More often than not, there will be one, though it might not be as well advertised as the main choices.

YOU ARE THE ONLY ONE RESPONSIBLE FOR YOUR DECISIONS

Sure, there will be people who may influence the choices you make but, ultimately, you are the person who made those choices. Be sure to recognize that and own up to those decisions, whether they were right or wrong.

One of the quickest ways to lose the respect of your peers is to constantly blame others for the decisions you made. Take the blame when you're wrong and, just as important, take credit when you are right.

YOUR FINANCIAL SITUATION CAN CHANGE FASTER THAN YOU REALIZE

If you reach a point where you are earning enough to live comfortably, don't take it for granted. Make sure to stash money in a savings account for emergencies and be fiscally responsible in general. If life does throw you a curveball, remember it is OK to take a job to pay the bills, even if it may seem beneath you, until you get back on your feet. Don't let your pride result in you losing the roof over your head.

IT IS POSSIBLE TO MAKE THE RIGHT DECISION AND STILL HATE IT

This happens a lot more often than you would think and always stinks, especially if the decision ends up hurting someone you care about. It is, however, often unavoidable.

The best way to avoid losing sleep over this is to focus on why you made the decision rather than the decision itself. There will likely still be a sting but it helps if you are able to reassure yourself the decision was made for the right reasons.

THE BEST SOLUTION ISN'T ALWAYS THE MOST PRACTICAL ONE

Sometimes, you can come up with the perfect solution to a problem on paper but won't be able to accomplish it when the real-world obstacles are factored in (most of the time, it will be a money issue).

When this happens, you are going to need to be willing to compromise and go with the second or even third best option. It might not be the perfect answer but can still be considered a win.

PUNCTUALITY IS AN EASY WAY TO MAKE A GOOD FIRST IMPRESSION

Whether you are meeting a person for business or social reasons, treat their time as a gift and show the proper respect by not arriving late. If circumstances prevent this, then at least make an effort to reach out to the person to let them know. Along the same lines, don't forget good manners matter too. "Please" and "thank you" go a long way toward making that first impression a good one.

DON'T RESPOND TO DRAMA WITH MORE DRAMA

This probably won't be easy, especially if you feel like you were wronged. However, drama doesn't deescalate on its own and, unless you want to waste a good chunk of your life in a never-ending and unproductive cycle, it's best to take a deep breath and be the one who takes that first step toward getting things to calm down.
Even if you can't be the voice of reason, at least try to be the cooler head.

LEARN WHEN TO BITE YOUR TONGUE

Sometimes it is best to just keep your mouth shut, especially when emotions are running high, and wait for a situation to play itself out. That way, if you still feel the need to give your two cents, you'll have all the information and will have given yourself time to fine tune what you are going to say.

YOU HAVE TO TREAT SOME PEOPLE LIKE MAGICIANS

If they are telling you to focus your attention on one thing, make sure to keep your eyes open and look for the thing they don't want you to notice.
This is especially true of many politicians but you'd be surprised by the number of people you'll encounter that this will apply to.

NEVER UNDERESTIMATE THE BENEFIT OF A SET ROUTINE

A little predictability goes a long way in an unpredictable world and having a set routine is a great way to navigate through life's challenges. While you should still be willing to be flexible, having a familiar schedule and habits will help you quickly get back to a sense of "normal" if things go awry and you find yourself feeling lost.

DON'T DISMISS THE HEALING BENEFIT OF SUNSHINE AND FRESH AIR

Obviously, these two things aren't a cure for everything. However, there are a lot of ailments in life that can be either lessened or cured simply by getting outdoors and taking advantage of the things Mother Nature gave us.

In fact, I highly recommend at least trying this treatment plan before resorting to pills and other things that might have potential side effects.

NOTHING IS IMPOSSIBLE BUT A LOT OF THINGS ARE IMPROBABLE

There is a chance you will win that big lottery jackpot but that doesn't mean you should base your retirement plans around that happening. The same can be said about a lot of other things in life.
It's OK to chase those improbable dreams. Just make sure you understand the odds and be willing to chase a more-achievable dream if those odds become even more unfavorable.

USE YOUR SICK DAYS

I'm not saying to call in sick when you have a hangnail but, if you are legitimately ill, take the time off that is needed to get you healthy again. You may not believe work can survive without you but chances are they can. If they can't, then that gives you a lot more leverage when you want that pay raise.

Also, don't forget about your vacation days. They have no value if they aren't used.

JUST BECAUSE YOU DON'T AGREE WITH SOMEONE DOESN'T MEAN YOU SHOULDN'T LISTEN TO WHAT THEY ARE SAYING

Sometimes people don't necessarily need you to agree with them, they just want to be heard. Listening closely to their arguments will help you see the issue from their point-of-view.
You may never completely agree with them but understanding their perspective will make it easier to feel empathy and bring you one step closer to finding some sort of common ground.

JUDGE YOUR SOCIAL LIFE BY QUALITY, NOT QUANTITY.

Having 100 friends doesn't mean a whole heck of a lot if 99 of them find excuses not to be there for you when you need them. It doesn't matter if you have a social circle that numbers in the single digits as long as you are associating with people who will have your back when you need them.

ADULTS SOMETIMES HAVE TO DO THINGS THEY DON'T LIKE WITH PEOPLE THEY DON'T LIKE

This is especially true if/when you become a parent and are forced to interact with other parents because of school activities, etc. As much as you'll want to avoid it, it eventually happens to everyone. There's not much I can give you for advice other than to make the best of it and do everything you can to make the experience end as quickly as possible.

IT IS HARD TO EARN SOMEONE'S TRUST BUT IT IS EVEN HARDER TO RE-EARN IT

Don't take someone else's trust for granted, especially if you are in a relationship with that person. If you violate that trust, whether it is on purpose or not, you may still be friends/more with that person but the relationship will never be quite the same afterwards. In other words, don't take what you have for granted.

YOUR BODY HAS ZERO TRADE-IN VALUE

Don't be afraid to put as many miles on it as you can by seeing the world or getting a little wear and tear by trying new activities.

Eventually, when you're older, you'll have all sorts of aches and pains (it happens to everyone). Those aches and pains are a lot more tolerable if they come with fond memories.

A LOT OF THINGS GO UNCHANGED IN THIS WORLD BECAUSE EVERYONE IS WAITING FOR SOMEONE ELSE TO DO IT

You should never feel as though you are responsible for solving all the world's problems but if an opportunity presents itself, you should step up. Sure, there's a chance someone else will eventually do it if you don't, but you shouldn't count on that happening.

TURN OFF THE LIGHTS WHEN YOU DON'T NEED THEM

Yeah, I know, this sounds like the stereotypical "dad" statement. However, this is more than just about saving money on your electric bill.

For the foreseeable future, a large percentage of our electricity is going to come from sources that aren't so good for the environment. And, you never know, maybe today's "clean" energy sources aren't as good for the planet as we think.

Do Mother Nature a favor and make sure you aren't using any more electricity than you absolutely need to. All it takes is a flip of a switch.

DON'T TREAT PEOPLE THE WAY YOU THINK THEY DESERVE

Instead, treat them in a way that will let you go to bed at night knowing you are a good person. Giving someone their comeuppance feels good in the moment, but consistently getting a guilt-free sleep feels a whole lot better and is better for you.

MAKE HISTORY ONE OF YOUR HOBBIES

Studying history is a bit like a sports team studying game film. It gives you an opportunity to better understand mankind's achievements and failures, especially if you take the time to look at things from multiple points of view.

When applied to current events, an understanding of history can make it easier to know when things will likely be OK and when it is time to start worrying.

BE A LEADER, BUT ALSO BE WILLING TO BE A FOLLOWER

Everyone wants to be the person in charge and, if the opportunity presents itself, you should take full advantage of it. However, also remain humble enough to accept when someone else is obviously more qualified than you for that role. Give that person the loyalty and support you would expect if you were in their shoes.

LOYALTY ISN'T ALWAYS RECIPROCATED

It is OK to be loyal to a friend, a romantic partner, an employer, etc. Just make sure that loyalty isn't too one-sided. One of the worst feelings in the world is giving a person (or job) everything you have only to find out they view you as easily replaceable.

DON'T BE TOO PROUD TO ACCEPT HELP WHEN YOU NEED IT

We all hit rough patches in our lives and, sometimes, it can feel embarrassing or even degrading to accept someone's offer to help us through those bad times.

If you need help, whether it is buying a meal or a shoulder to cry on, don't turn down those who are offering it to you. Once you get back on your feet, there will be plenty of opportunities for you to pay it forward.

BE WILLING TO "EDIT" YOUR LIFE

If you don't like the way an essay sounds when writing it, you change it to make it better. You can do the same with your life.

Start by removing all negative people from your circle of "friends," followed by any unnecessary activity that isn't enjoyable and is a drain on your time and/or your bank account.

If needed, it is never too late to do a full rewrite. Just make sure to do it in a way that allows you to retrieve the important parts of your previous "draft."

THE BEST REVENGE IS SIMPLY CUTTING PEOPLE OUT OF YOUR LIFE

It's the best of both worlds. You are punishing them by denying an opportunity to enjoy the good things you have to offer without the stress of coming up with the "perfect" way to get back at them.
Your life is too short to waste on people who honestly just aren't worth it.

THERE IS A FINE LINE BETWEEN BEING CONFIDENT AND PEOPLE THINKING YOU'RE POMPOUS

It is OK to show you are confident in your abilities. Just remember you want the people around you to notice that confidence and embrace it. If you take things too far, those same people will think of you as arrogant and will want you to fail. Pay attention to their reactions and, if needed, tone it down a bit.

JUST BECAUSE A TOPIC OF CONVERSATION DOESN'T SOUND IMPORTANT DOESN'T MEAN IT ISN'T IMPORTANT TO THE PERSON YOU'RE TALKING TO

Treat all topics of conversation with a reasonable amount of respect, even if it is a subject you may not have any real interest in. You would, after all, expect the same courtesy if you were talking about something you cared deeply about.

SOME PEOPLE WILL VIEW YOUR ACHIEVEMENTS AS THEIR FAILURES

They will become jealous and upset. They may even say hurtful things in an effort to take away from your success. The thing to remember is it is their problem, not yours. Don't let another person's negativity make you feel guilty about what you accomplished.

On the flip side of this, always try to be supportive when other people have success. You'll be much happier in the end.

THE END OF THE WORLD SELLS AD SPACE

I'm not saying things aren't bad or will never be bad, it's just that they are rarely as bad as the media wants you to believe. Bad news gets people to click an article or video link and the badder the news, the better.
Instead of letting this get you down, learn to read between the lines and how to separate fact from exaggeration.

NOBODY EVER ACHIEVED GREATNESS BY DOING THE BARE MINIMUM

Always try to put in a little extra with everything you do, even if it is something that might seem menial. You may not always see a benefit from the extra work but people who don't do more than is absolutely necessary are pretty much guaranteeing themselves a subpar existence.

NEVER RISK MORE THAN YOU ARE WILLING TO LOSE

This is great gambling advice but is also great life advice. There will be times in your life when you will be offered opportunities that require you to risk something important, like job security or even a relationship. Be sure to understand those risks and take a moment or two to decide if the opportunity is worth losing something of value to you.

INVEST IN YOURSELF

Whether you're taking a class to learn a new skill or joining a gym to stay in shape, look at the money/time being spent as investing in the person you are today and want to be tomorrow.
Even something as simple as a new hairstyle or wardrobe update can be considered an investment if they will make you a more confident person and you should never feel guilty for putting yourself first.

LET PEOPLE TELL THEIR OWN STORY

Simply put, if something isn't about you or doesn't involve you, it's not your story to tell. Don't start or repeat gossip and don't believe everything you hear about someone unless that person is giving you the information first-hand.

The world would be a much better place if everyone respected a person's right to share their narrative in their own words. Don't be part of the problem.

AVOIDING A CHORE IS SOMETIMES MORE WORK THAN JUST DOING IT

This obviously isn't always going to be the case but if you ever find yourself doing a bunch of extra work to avoid doing a job you don't want to do, ask yourself if it would just be simpler/faster to just do the task you are avoiding.

TAKE PLENTY OF PHOTOS

And keep them where they are easily accessible. You never know when you'll need a visual reminder of a happy day or a long-passed loved one. Having lots of photos of your adventures and your loved ones is a lot more comforting than a lot of people realize and many people, me included, regret not having them later in life.

ALWAYS CONSIDER YOURSELF A WORK IN PROGRESS

Don't rest on your laurels because there is always room for improvement. On the flip side of that, don't get down on yourself because of a set back because there is no reason to believe you won't be able to eventually overcome that obstacle with a little more time, knowledge and experience.
Also remember, change isn't always instantaneous. Sometimes it might take weeks, months, or even years for you to see the progress. Don't grow frustrated if it isn't happening at the pace you expected.

YOU WON'T BECOME A WISE PERSON UNLESS YOU MAKE MISTAKES

A large amount of wisdom is the direct result of overcoming your screw ups. Be sure to remember that and treat each mistake as the learning experience it is. This is also the reason you shouldn't let the fear of making a mistake stop you from trying something new.

LET OTHERS MAKE MISTAKES TOO

Sometimes the best way to teach someone something is to let them do it the wrong way first. This is especially true of children but applies to many adults as well, especially those who stubbornly refuse to ask for help.

This isn't always an easy thing to do, it is human nature to want to correct someone. It is, however, a necessity at times.

AVOID TAKING SIDES IN ARGUMENTS THAT DON'T INVOLVE YOU

You will be tempted to do this, especially if it involves a friend or someone you care about. However, picking sides can often cause more problems, especially if you only have one side of the story and/or are biased. You could even find yourself receiving some of the blame.

Be a shoulder for people to cry on but do your best not to take things any further than that.

IT'S EASY TO GIVE ADVICE WHEN YOU HAVE NOTHING AT STAKE

This ties in with what I just said about arguments but is important enough to justify its own entry. Things always seem less complicated from the outside looking in and "common sense" advice may not be as relevant to a particular situation as you may think.

As a general rule, if someone is going through something, don't give them advice unless you are asked. You may think you are helping, but you likely are making things even more difficult for them.

On the flip side of that, don't feel obligated to accept a friend's advice if you're going through something. They may mean well, but they aren't you.

IT IS NEVER TOO LATE TO WALK AWAY FROM TOXICITY

If you have a lot of time invested in something or someone, it might be difficult to find the courage to walk away, partly because you don't want to feel like that time was wasted.

Don't fall into that trap. If something or someone is causing you unneeded stress and/or making you feel like less of a person, walk away. Don't think of it as time wasted. Think of it as time spent learning what you don't need in your life.

IT'S NOT REALLY A GOOD PLAN UNLESS YOU INCLUDE THE LOGISTICS

Any competent general will tell you it doesn't matter if you have a larger army if you can't feed your soldiers or provide them with enough ammunition. Apply this same philosophy to your life choices, whether it is choosing where to stop for gas when taking a road trip with friends or figuring out how you are going to buy food while waiting for the first paycheck from a new job. It may not be the "fun" part of the plan but it will save you a lot of misery later.

DIVERSIFY YOUR JOY

Treat your happiness the same way you would treat a financial portfolio. The joy you receive from certain people and activities may wane over time and there might even be a time when those things bring you no joy at all. So, protect yourself by finding multiple things that bring you joy and be willing to add something new to the list every once in a while.

DON'T JUDGE PEOPLE BASED ON THEIR RELATIONSHIP STATUS (OR LACK OF ONE)

There is no "right" way to be in a relationship. Some couples enjoy being married. Others are perfectly happy being together without taking that step. There are even those who don't want a commitment of any kind. Don't let your own opinions of the perfect relationship cloud your judgment.

Also, just because someone is single doesn't mean there is something wrong with them. It just means they are either choosing to be happy by themselves or are waiting for the right person. Don't think less of them.

This advice also applies to your opinion of yourself. Don't let your own relationship status influence what you think of yourself.

THERE IS ALWAYS TIME TO READ

It may not always seem like it, especially when you're busy doing other things, but everyone has time to read a book, article, etc., as long as they are a bit creative.

Bring a book with you to read in a doctor's waiting room or keep a magazine handy for when you are making a call and are placed on hold. You'll be surprised by the number of pages you'll be able to read if you make productive use of otherwise unproductive time.

Also, try to read a variety of genres and subjects, especially from people with controversial viewpoints. It'll make you a better conversationalist.

LEARN TO "AGREE TO DISAGREE"

This is especially true of political and religious views. People have strong opinions and many friendships have been lost over attempts to change those opinions.

It's OK to have your own beliefs and it is OK if you don't agree with someone else's beliefs. Just don't let that difference of opinion be the reason an otherwise great relationship came to an end.

Along these same lines, sometimes it just isn't worth even engaging. Not every battle is worth fighting, so choose the ones that actually mean something.

IT IS DIFFICULT TO UNHEAR THINGS ONCE THEY ARE SAID

This is even more true today than it was when I was younger because just about everyone has some sort of recording device now. Take your time and think before you speak. Words said in the moment, especially when there is emotion involved, could follow you for a long time.

IMPORTANT DECISIONS ARE RARELY MADE IN A BUBBLE

Much more often than not, an important life choice is going to affect more than just you. It doesn't mean you shouldn't do (or not do) something. It just means you should at least attempt to be aware of this ripple effect so you aren't caught off guard by an unintended consequence.

THE ADAGE "CHEATERS NEVER PROSPER" IS A LIE

If it were true, you wouldn't have people still cheating.

However, cheating does usually come at some sort of price - the loss of friends/loved ones, a loss of respect and, in some cases, the possibility of a criminal record. You may even hate yourself for doing it..

It may not be as easy to do things honestly, especially if others are cheating to get ahead of you, but don't underestimate just how good it feels to look in a mirror and not think less of yourself because you took that easier route.

A SURPRISING NUMBER OF THINGS ARE OPEN TO INTERPRETATION

Just because you have facts that support your claim, don't assume someone couldn't look at those same facts and interpret them another way. One person's hero is another person's villain and plenty of other things can be taken in a different context based on someone's point of view.

JUST BECAUSE SOMETHING IS "OLD SCHOOL" DOESN'T MEAN IT ISN'T AS VALUABLE

A smartphone with GPS is awesome, but a road map doesn't require a signal or charged battery. A paper advertisement on a well-placed community bulletin board will be just as effective as posting an event on social media.

Just because there are newer ways to do things doesn't mean the old-fashioned ways didn't work or should be dismissed. A new approach isn't necessarily always the best approach.

JUST BECAUSE SOMETHING IS CONSIDERED A "CLASSIC" DOESN'T MEAN YOU ARE OBLIGATED TO LIKE IT

People tend to see the past through rose-colored glasses. This is especially true when it comes to "classic" books, movies or music.

While you should respect and appreciate these things for their historical and cultural value, feel free to judge them for yourself and don't feel guilty if you don't enjoy them as much as others. Chances are, you aren't alone in that opinion.

INTELLIGENCE IS RELATIVE

Even if, on paper, you are the most intelligent person in the room, there is likely someone there that knows something you don't. Don't dismiss another person's ideas or opinions based on their level of education. Practical experience will always trump things that are learned in a classroom.

YOU CAN LEARN A LOT OF LIFE LESSONS WATCHING HORROR FILMS

Shortcuts can be dangerous. Don't be a bully. Poor decisions can come back to haunt you years later. Respect other people's property. A safe/boring choice is often better than the more exciting choice. Always know where the emergency exit is. Learn self defense. Wear sensible shoes.

The list is practically endless so, when watching, take notes.

DON'T FORGET TO SHOWER

This sounds like an easy one, along with "don't forget to sleep" and "don't forget to eat." However, life can sometimes get a bit crazy and, when that happens, it is surprisingly easy to forget to take care of yourself.

No matter what life throws at you, make sure your health, hygiene and other basic needs receive priority over everything else. It may not seem like it at the time, but there is nothing more important than those things.

SUCCESS IS NOT A ONE-PERSON SHOW

Behind every successful person is a group of people who helped in their own way. This could be your parents, your friends, your co-workers, or even someone you don't even know exists.

If you are fortunate enough to achieve one or more of your dreams, make sure you don't forget about those people. You wouldn't have gotten where you are without their sacrifices.

EACH MORNING YOU WAKE UP, BE PROUD OF YOURSELF FOR BEING A SURVIVOR

The world is a scary place and you could fill a set of encyclopedias with the various ways it could kill you, including something as simple as choking on a piece of your favorite food or catching the common cold.
Be proud of your survival instincts and pat yourself on the back everytime you live to see the sun rise.

BREATHE

Adulthood can be difficult and overwhelming. There will be days when you'll feel lost, days when you'll be frustrated, and days when you'll wonder if maybe you should just give up.

When this happens, pause and breathe. Will it solve all your problems? No. It will, however, give you a chance to regroup and realize, no matter the situation, you can handle it.

Made in United States
North Haven, CT
26 March 2024

50519927R00059